AF269724

JUST DANCE

Spotlight on Stepping

Mel Hammond

Lerner Publications ◆ Minneapolis

Lerner Publications Company
An imprint of Lerner Publishing Group, Inc.
241 First Avenue North
Minneapolis, MN 55401 USA

For reading levels and more information, look up this title at www.lernerbooks.com.

Main body text set in Mikado.
Typeface provided by HVD.

Designer: Mary Ross

Library of Congress Cataloging-in-Publication Data

Names: Hammond, Mel, author.
Title: Spotlight on stepping / Mel Hammond.
Description: Minneapolis, MN : Lerner Publications, [2025] | Series: Lerner sports rookie. Just dance | Includes bibliographical references and index. | Audience: Ages 5–8 | Audience: Grades K–1 | Summary: "Get ready to stomp, step, and clap! Readers discover stepping from its beginnings in Black communities to how people perform and celebrate this type of dance today. Then learn a specific move!"– Provided by publisher.
Identifiers: LCCN 2023048885 (print) | LCCN 2023048886 (ebook) | ISBN 9798765625682 (library binding) | ISBN 9798765628867 (paperback) | ISBN 9798765634127 (epub)
 Subjects: LCSH: African American dance–Juvenile literature.
   Classification: LCC GV1624.7.A34 H36 2025 (print) | LCC GV1624.7.A34 (ebook) | DDC 793.3–dc23/eng/20231122

LC record available at https://lccn.loc.gov/2023048885
LC ebook record available at https://lccn.loc.gov/2023048886

Manufactured in the United States of America
1-1010141-51902-2/7/2024

Table of Contents

Chapter 1

Step In

Get ready to stomp, step, and clap! Stepping is a type of dance. It began in Africa.

From 1619 to 1865, many Black people in the US were enslaved. They couldn't use the drums that were part of their traditions. They stepped instead.

★ Fun Fact ★
Today's step dancers celebrate Black history by stepping.

Getting Ready

Steppers practice in stretchy clothes to help them move. They usually wear sneakers.

9

Dancers make their own music by stomping
and clapping. Sometimes dancers also sing.

What to Expect

At practice, steppers stretch.
They do exercises to warm up.

The coach teaches a step. Everyone practices it. The team learns more steps. Then they put the moves together.

★ **Tip** ★

Different claps make different sounds. Try clapping with your hands flat or cupped.

16

★ Up Close! ★

Do an Over-Under

- Stomp one of your legs.
- Lift your other leg.
- Clap your hands above the lifted leg.
- Clap your hands below the lifted leg.
- Repeat the steps on the other side.

Putting on a Show

Steppers can perform anywhere. Watch them at schools, churches, outdoors, and competitions.

★ Fun Fact ★
Beyoncé has stepped during some of her concerts!

Steppers wear matching clothes.
Some teams wear T-shirts and jeans.
Others wear colorful costumes.

Stepping is exciting. Now it's your turn!

TEP AFRIKA

Glossary

competition: an event where someone tries to win something that someone else is also trying to win

cupped: shaped like a cup

enslaved: not free and forced to work without pay or rights

tradition: a way of thinking or doing something that has been done for a long time

Learn More

Bode, Heather L. *Dance.* Minneapolis: Early Encyclopedias, 2024.

Isdahl, Nansubuga Nagadya. *Beyoncé.* New York: Abrams Books for Young Readers, 2021.

Peters, Katie. *Dance: A First Look.* Minneapolis: Lerner Publications, 2023.

Index

Photo Acknowledgments

Image credits: Martha Asencio-Rhine/Tampa Bay Times via ZUMA Press Wire/Alamy, p. 5; Jon Cherry/Getty Images, p. 7; Liz Condo/AP Images for Sprite, p. 9; Roger Kisby/Getty Images, pp. 11, 21; Drazen Zigic/Shutterstock, p. 13; Tony Avelar/AP Images for Sprite, p. 15; Kathryn Scott/The Denver Post via Getty Images, p. 16; Tim Brown/Alamy, p. 17; Kevin Mazur/Getty Images for Coachella, p. 19; St. Petersburg Times/ZUMApress.com/Alamy, p. 23. Design elements: Kilroy79/Getty Images, Iuliia Mashinets/Getty Images.

Cover: Liz Condo/AP Images for Sprite.